HERMETIC
DEFINITION

by H.D.

A NEW DIRECTIONS BOOK

Parts of some of the poems included in this collection were first published
in *Contemporary Literature, Evergreen Review* and *The Nation*.

Sections 13 and 14 of "Sagesse" first appeared in *Poetry* as "Regents of
the Night."

First published clothbound and as New Directions Paperbook 343
in 1972
Published simultaneously in Canada by McClelland & Stewart, Ltd.
Manufactured in the United States of America

New Directions Books are published for James Laughlin
by New Directions Publishing Corporation,
333 Sixth Avenue, New York 10014

FOREWORD

Remembering, H.D. wrote of September 1912: "In London in fall, mist and fog. E.P. in B.M. tea-shop says, Hermes, Orchard, Acon will 'do.'" They did — for many years in the public mind and for some critics still. But for H.D., the early manner of her Imagist poems was inadequate. Poems like her war trilogy — *The Walls Do Not Fall*, *Tribute to the Angels*, and *The Flowering of the Rod* — and the hitherto unpublished poems in *Hermetic Definition* go beyond what her early admirers referred to as crystalline. They retain the energy that goes into the essence of gems, but in a deeper, more probing daemonic drive that carried her through old mysteries into new life.

What had been chiefly Greek metaphor became increasingly myth, joined by Egyptian parallels and memories of the Moravian background of her childhood. "The spirit caught back into the old mysteries of Egypt and Greece," she wrote. When I took her home to Bethlehem, Pennsylvania, she stood in the aisle of the Central Church, remembering love feasts and the Unitas Fratrum. She was fascinated by Zinzendorf and his re-establishment of "a branch of the dispersed or 'lost' Church of Provence, the Church of Love that we touch on in *By Avon River*." It was not casual when, as we left the church, she signed the Register and added "Baptized Moravian."

She had learned to tell the stories of the stars and constellations when she showed visiting schoolchildren the heavens through the telescope of the Flower Observatory, near Philadelphia, where her father was astronomer. Visits to Greece and to Egypt deepened her knowledge. A sense of fuller significance came later.

Freud was a significant tutor. As E. B. Butler, a friend, wrote in answer to a letter from her, "I entirely agree about him: a great mythologist to whom we all owe an incalculable debt on the poetic side." As H.D. herself wrote elsewhere, "Without the analysis and the illuminating doctrine or philosophy of Sigmund Freud, I would hardly have found the clue or the bridge between the child-life, the memories of peaceful Bethlehem and the orgy of destruction, later to be witnessed and lived through in London. That outer threat and constant reminder of death drove me inward. . . ." The war was both tutor and goad; with it she began a new period of creativity.

What Freud gave her was a sense of how to link the tribal myths with the personal dream, and to help her understand multiple representations of inner drives. Like Yeats and like Pound, both friends, she could be comprehensive in her reference. Living as she did in Switzerland, she was accustomed to moving back and forth between English, German, and French in her conversation. Living in literature, she could equally move between myths and metaphors of multiple cultures, understanding with what relevance they could be interchanged. Like many Freudians, she became quasi-Jungian and could bring the cabala, astrology, magic, Christianity, classical and Egyptian mythology, and personal experience into a joint sense of Ancient Wisdom.

This sense of "ancient wisdom" is what "hermetic definition" is. "Isis takes many forms, as does Osiris," she says. H.D. had her core myth, certain that "women are individually seeking, as one woman, fragments of the Eternal Lover. As the Eternal Lover has been scattered or dissociated, so she in her search for him. In *Bid Me to Live* (*A Madrigal*), she seeks for him in contemporary time. . . . She seeks him in fantasy, myth." So she puts it.

So she also puts it in the three long poems of *Hermetic Definition*. The title piece is such a search, built on fantasy and myth, but none the less real or meaningful because chance encounters are made legendary. Robert Ambelain's *Dans l'ombre des cathédrales* (1939) is a ring of keys to references. Her copy was well marked. The book has to do with the Christianization of hermeticism, or vice versa as one prefers. In any event, its scheme permits a liaison between Christian symbolism as evidenced in the decoration of the portals of Notre Dame and traditional hermetic schemes like those lingering from Isis and Bar-Isis, her son. The rose is not only the rose which unfolds slowly in Ezra Pound's Canto 106 but the Rose-Croix as well, and all symbolic roses. Lines in French from Ambelain interweave with lines from Saint-John Perse's *Exil* and *Anabase*. The figure of the chief of the Paris Bureau of *Newsweek*, a Haitian, blends with that of Perse and of Rafer Johnson, the decathlon star who reminded her of Olympia. Lionel Durand saw H.D. only twice: in April 1960 in Switzerland, where he had come to interview her after the publication of *Bid Me to Live*, and in May in New York, where she had gone to receive the gold medal for poetry awarded by the American Academy of Arts and Letters. He died of a heart attack nine months after they first met. She briefly thought of calling the poem "Notre-Dame d'Amour"; Durand was simply a member of the congregation whose reality was myth.

Perse she met only at the ceremony where the medal was presented. She had broken her hip in 1956, and never again could walk except with difficulty. Sitting behind her chair, he reached out to help her. As H.D. wrote me later, she remembered "the gallant Léger Léger's gesture as I staggered — no swayed gracefully — from the reader's desk" where she had made her speech of acceptance. But mostly she remembered that they were, both, poets. The crowded Academy was the Grove of Academe, to balance the solitude of the room at Küsnacht where resin and pine-cone significantly burned. The final section, "Star of Day," is one of death and rebirth: the poet as seeker now become mother, fecund in the creation of still another fragment of the recurrent myth.

"Sagesse" is a hermetic definition, an owl as of Athena, and "Owl Calendrier Sacré" or "Heures Sacrées" to give the poem's alternative titles that define what H.D. was after.

The circumstances were those of her broken hip and long hours abed. Ambelain figures again. This time it is his *La Kabbale pratique* (1951) to which one can turn for definitions. More conveniently, one can use Gustav Davidson's *A Dictionary of Angels* (1967), which includes the references in "Sagesse." "At one time," H.D. wrote, "I studied intimately Robert Ambelain's long list of presiding angels. There are three for each hour. Thus, there would be about twelve for the night hours between 2 and Dawn when I can not sleep." "I try to write in bed," she wrote Richard Aldington, her former husband, "the few letters, the odd poems. The poems are about an *Owl*, 'a captive and in prison.'" She herself felt captive and imprisoned at Küsnacht, on Lake Zürich, cared for by Schwester Annie and the other nurses, visited occasionally by another patient, and watched over by a German doctor on the staff much interested and a little puzzled by her poems.

The occasion was a picture of an owl in the London zoo, published in *The Listener* for May 9, 1957. "I began the poem, June 9th," she wrote me. "I get *Listener* late, and often don't look over the copies for some time." There were echoes in the caged bird of Pound in Pisa and at St. Elizabeth's Hospital. Even more there was, as I have said, herself caged. There was herself looking at herself. There was the balancing imagined little girl at the zoo looking at the owl.

> May those who file before you feel
> something of what you are — that God is kept within
> the narrow confines of a cage, a pen. . . .

The poem plays back and forth between the scenes of the child and her family in London, and the scenes in the sanitarium at Küsnacht. The German questions; he is Germain also: an echo of the eighteenth-century magician and contemporary of Cagliostro and Casanova whom she had introduced as a character with his own mystery in her as-yet-unpublished Moravian novel, *The Mystery*. "Sagesse" is a poem of the spirit at night, before dawn and the rising sun. The guardian angels, the *sentiers*, must be sought. "I am glad," she wrote me, "there is the 'laugh the world away' feeling at the end."

Midwinter and spring of 1959 were given to "Winter Love." "I am doing short *Helen* poems," she wrote me in February, "a sequence, though hardly a *Canto* or 'big poem.' It keeps the connection with the original 'the early H.D.' too." In April, "I am deep in *Espérance*, a short sequence — I connect the title with your *Sagesse* choice. This is helping me." And in May, she "started to type the *Espérance*, which I think I now call, *Winter Love*. Some of the poems are done in a strangely familiar, Swinburnian metre — I can't think that I *must* be Pound-Eliot."

"Winter Love" was, as she often referred to it, a "Coda" to *Helen in Egypt*, picking up once more all that her Helens have from the beginning expressed in terms of the quest. "Winter Love" is a poem "in contemporary time," her own older age. When *Helen in Egypt* (1961) was published, I wished to include "Winter Love" as an actual coda. It would, it seemed to me, by bringing the legend on down in time, show how she herself had always figured in her own poems. If she was true to the Greeks, she was true to the Greek in herself. H.D. agreed that "Winter Love" could be included. Then, just before the manuscript finally went in, she changed her mind. Its appearance in the same book would, she felt, destroy the poem she had originally conceived. For although her poems are personal, they are never purely personal. They are part of something very much larger than herself. Her "self-seeking quest" was for the encompassing "self" of which she was only a part.

NORMAN HOLMES PEARSON

New Haven
May 1972

CONTENTS

CONTENTS

HERMETIC DEFINITION

PART ONE

Red Rose and a Beggar

(August 17 – September 24, 1960)

[1]

Why did you come
to trouble my decline?
I am old (I was old till you came);

the reddest rose unfolds,
(which is ridiculous
in this time, this place,

unseemly, impossible,
even slightly scandalous),
the reddest rose unfolds;

(nobody can stop that,
no immanent threat from the air,
not even the weather,

blighting our summer fruit),
the reddest rose unfolds,
(they've got to take that into account).

Take me anywhere, anywhere;
I walk into you,
Doge — Venice —

you are my whole estate;
I would hide in your mind
as a child hides in an attic,

what would I find there?
religion or majic — both? neither?
one or the other? together, matched,

mated, exactly the same,
equal in power, together yet separate,
your eyes' amber.

Isis, Iris,
fleur-de-lis,
Bar-Isis is son of Isis,

(bar ou ber ou ben, signifiant fils),
so Bar-Isis is Par-Isis?
Paris, anyway;

because you do not drink our wine,
nor salt our salt,
I would enter your senses

through burnt resin and pine-cones
smouldering in a flat dish;
were you a cave-hermit?

why do they punish us?
come out, come out of the darkness;
will I be burnt to cinders in this heat?

They say the hieratic and heraldic iris
is the lotus, martigan-lily,
magenta, purple — do I blaspheme?

cowering under the rain,
I think of the hot sand,
and call and call again

Bar-Isis, Paris;
I call Paris, Paris,
not to the Greek

nor to the courtly suitor of Verona
"where we lay our scene,"
though Verona is not far,

now I walk into you,
Doge — Venice —
you are my whole estate.

Venice — Venus?
this must be my stance,
my station: though you brushed aside

my verse,
I can't get away from it,
I've tried to;

true, it was "fascinating . . .
if you can stand its preciousness,"
you wrote of what I wrote;

why must I write?
you would not care for this,
but She draws the veil aside,

unbinds my eyes,
commands,
write, write or die.

This is my new prayer;
I pray to you?
Paris, Bar-Isis? to Osiris?

or to Isis-self, Egyptian flower,
Notre Dame — do you ever go there?
the stones hold secrets;

they tell us vibration was brought over
by ancient alchemists;
Our Lady keeps tryst,

she commands with her sceptre, (*Astrologie*
is the first door?)
and the Child champions us;

bid me not despair,
Child of the ancient hierarchy
and you to-day.

Saint Anne is the last door, (Magie,
Cybele, they once called her,
the grand-mother),

and where are we now?
certainly there is the rush, the fervour,
the trampling of lush grass,

the bare feet entanglement,
the roar of the last desperate charge,
the non-escape, the enchantment,

the tremor, the earthquake,
nothing, nothing, nothing more,
nothing further; the pine-cone

we left smouldering in the flat dish,
is flaming, is fire,
no before, no after — escape?

who can escape life, fever,
the darkness of the abyss?
lost, lost, lost,

the last desperate non-escape,
the reddest rose,
the unalterable law . . . . .

is it you?
is it some thundering pack
of steers, bulls? is it one?

is it many?
voices from the past, from the future,
so far, no further,

now total abasement;
were you ever here?
were you ever in this room?

how did I endure your presence,
and afterwards, just once,
in a strange place, with others there,

silly talk, mine,
and you wouldn't drink our wine,
("then fruit-juice?" "yes"),

and you wouldn't touch our salt —
almonds — pecans — what happened?
you were so late,

why didn't you come sooner?
why did you come at all?
why did you come

to trouble my decline,
I am old,
(I was old till you came.)

The middle door is Judgement, (*Alchimie*),
judge this, judge me implacable;
there is yet time to crawl back

to security? no — there is no time left:
almonds, pecans without salt,
scatter them near some sand-coast

for a wind-break, beyond is the wax flower,
the thyme, honeymyrtle and the coral heath,
these are new to me, different,

as you are new to me, different,
but of an old, old sphere;
there are some small wild dogroses, I think,

but all this is nothing
when the desert wind bears the white
gumblossom eucalypts' fragrance;

no, no, this is too much,
we can not escape to a new continent;
the middle door is judgement,

I am judged — prisoner?
the reddest rose unfolds,
can I endure this?

Because you can not drink our wine
nor eat our salt,
(I asked "do you like salt?"

you said, "yes,") I keep remembering
my glass of red wine; one glass every day
becomes an orgy,

greed devours me,
wine is the sacrament,
salt has not lost its savour;

savour? saviour?
this is a new intensity,
but you are far away,

not so far — Paris;
hidden on or under a transept cross-bar,
the *Notre Dame* dedication is enigmatic,

each of the 18 Latin words has a double sense,
they tell us; I find *Secondo*, the 7th word,
means *Seconde, aide, et favorise*

l'action de la Nature . . .
and this was inscribed in 1257;
I think we will go far,

going nowhere; Cybele
(*Cybèle*, they write it),
is set over the last door.

It is heart,
this no-salt, they say,
you might go at any moment,

but that might be said of any of us,
so I must stand apart, keep away;
an intimate of my youth,

a poet wrote,
so slow is the rose to open,
so I contemplate these words

and the Latin dedication,
and would decipher my own fate;
I know the poet that I speak of

wouldn't hesitate,
perhaps humility is more becoming
in a woman;

la rose est la fleur du creuset,
and the *creuset* is the crucible
that I called a flat dish when I wrote [3],

I would enter your senses
through burnt resin
and pine-cones.

. . . but I must finish what I have begun
the tall god standing
where the race is run;

did the pine-cones in the flat dish
light an Olympic torch?
my fever, fervour was for one not born

when I wrote this;
the Red-Roses-for-Bronze
roses were for an abstraction;

now with like fervour, with fever,
I offer them to a reality;
the ecstasy comes through you

but goes on;
the torch was lit from another before you,
and another and another before that . . .

We leave the old bronze doors, 1257,
for another bronze, 1960,
I am thinking of the young athlete

with the spear, the poised javelin
as I saw him in the picture,
"U. S. Decathlon star,"

there is living bronze there,
the vibration of sun, desperate endeavour,
ambition, achievement, simplicity,

sheer strength reaching sublimity,
goodness that we might emulate,
(I might, at any rate),

"I like people,
I want to do all I can to help them,
in whatever little way I can,"

we can not compete
but perhaps we meet somewhere;
I with my seven-string lyre,

seem helpless, effete,
but where there is Olympia, Delphi is not far,
sublimation, recognition,

the very aspect of the Decathlon
slays desperation, as long ago (to-day)
Helios slays the Python.

So my *Red Roses for Bronze* (1930)
bring me to-day, a prophecy,
so these lyrics that would only embarrass you,

perhaps reach further into the future;
if it took 30 years for my *Red Roses for Bronze*
to find the exact image,

perhaps in 30 years,
life's whole complexity will be annulled,
when this *reddest rose unfolds*;

I won't be here,
probably you won't either;
in the meantime, there is beauty and valour

in these contests and passionate excitement as well,
and who was I to shrug and pass them by?
perhaps it was my "preciousness,"

as you called it,
but that was long ago,
last April,

and last May
when you came so late, in a strange place,
with others there.

The poet of *so slow is the rose to open*
writes, "what have I done with my life?"
what have I done with mine?

I stand again on the threshold,
on my left are the angels Astaroth, Lilith,
on my right, Raphael, Michael;

Astar — a star — Lili — a flower —
Raphael, Michael — why are you there?
would you guide me with dignity

into a known port?
would you champion my endeavour?
Astaroth, you can not be malign

with so beautiful a name,
have you brought me here?
Lilith, why do they call you a devil

with Lucifer and Asmodel?
true the *noms démoniaques* are
donnés sous toutes réserves :

Sesame
seed,
string
minute granules
on a white thread
or red,
will they split
on my needle?
do I need a thimble?
sesame
seed
from South Asia,
that is far away,
what comes between?
hemp — seed,
fleur de chanvre,
from India?
that is the *hachish supérieur*
of dream;
is it better to string
poppy-seeds?
they are too small;
they worshipped the Stars
on the top of the towers,
dites tours à parfums:

I need no rosary
of sesame,
only the days' trial,
reality . . .
faint,
faint,
faint,
O scent of roses
in this room.

[17]

O most august
and sacred host,
so do I turn and fade,

a candle in your light,
burnt to the quick;
you know I offered you my best,

hours, minutes, days, years spent
to proffer a small grain
of worship, incense,

my last breath (I thought)
to assemble in my song,
lines competent to praise,

of shame no taint, no *noms démoniaques*
invoked, no fallen angel
called by name;

19

now I am forced to hold my lines in doubt,
give me the answer,
let me know your grace,

whose is the Judgement?
there is One
indifferent to the realm of time and space,

Azrael; ironic and subtle in his smile,
near and familiar in his face,
(are his eyes amber?)

"is this your throw with Death?
right, left?
win, lose?

you court the end?
you call this life?
your rose so red

is bondage, stamp and seal,
you asked, 'I am judged prisoner?'
you spoke of Asmodel,

your rose so red
withers in any case,
renouncement? *feu d'enfer*?

now choose,
right, left,
win, lose."

Azrael said,
"you spoke of Asmodel,"
as if in reproval,

and I am temporarily astray;
I can't find Asmodel
in dictionary or reference book,

certainly not in the Saints' calendar;
Azrael is the Mohammedan angel of Death,
but we know that;

should we delete Asmodel
and find another?
who is he, anyway?

angels may become devils,
devils may become angels,
he'd better stay;

I must keep my identity,
walk unfalteringly toward a Lover,
the *hachish supérieur* of dream.

PART TWO

Grove of Academe

(November 1 – December 24, 1960)

[1]

So you (this other) are the Presence
in the Aegina temple,
at the top of the hill;

how could I have known this?
I could not have known it sooner,
I had to experience

the *roses, pourpre délice*
and the *roseraies de roses rouges*
before actually realizing

the wild-rose
precision, definition,
image of divination;

you are my own age,
my own stars;
I accepted acclaim

from the others,
for the honour,
unexpectedly thrust upon me,

some thousands were there,
then the Great Hall was empty,
though no one had moved away,

and I might have fallen
but your hand reached out to me,
and it was the *grove of academe*.

I read of initiations, adepts, neophites,
masters and imperators,
but this isn't it,

nor angels' names, nor right or wrong,
nor intricate *sentiers* or paths,
it's that you write,

even that I have written;
what is miraculous? I don't know,
it just happened,

it wasn't that I was accepted
by the State, the Office, the Assembly,
but by you;

it has taken some time
to realize the implication,
and much came between,

and whatever happened
is too simple to be written;
if I had hidden as I wanted to,

fearing acclaim,
I wouldn't have met you;
I do not disregard the others,

and there is nothing visionary
nor ecstatic here,
only recognition;

your mind's thought and range
exceeds mine
out of all proportion,

and indeed your words are esoteric
and difficult enough sometimes,
but exhausted by the whirlwind,

the storm of your poem's dimension,
I am the more stricken
when as a gift proffered,

you grant a moment's breathing-space,
cette grâce, par instants
and a *dahlia blanc*, that snow-owl

I did not cheat
nor fake inspiration,
what I wrote was right then,

auguries, hermetic definition;
yet, I would have left initiates, many times,
for a red rose and a beggar,

but something sustained me,
and when you greeted me,
I was paid fully

for the long search
and the meagre lamp;
there was no ecstasy, vision, trance,

no years between,
only an end to the whole adventure,
it stops here;

there is no striving for strange ships,
Adamic delights;
I have tasted the apple;

my hand worn with endeavour,
our curious pre-occupation with stylus and pencil,
was re-born at your touch.

No one has known her,
has shown her as you,
no other stood alone

to slay the Monster;
there is one Perseus,
unchallenged, an exile,

no one strung snow-flakes
for a white rosary,
nor invoked umbels,

virgin flower-clusters for her,
nor compelled her Presence
with the great *Ave de grâce*;

if I can do nothing else,
at least, I can recognize this
unfathomable, dauntless separation,

this retreat from the world,
that yet holds the world, past, present,
in the mind's closed recess;

suffice — where am I?
the "other side" where you always were,
with no cloudy ghost-convoy,

no majic, *Seigneur*,
but infinite mystery,
wind, sand, rain and snow

(her white rosary),
with the Owl,
her confederate.

Is remembrance chiefly a matter
of twig, leaf, grass, stone?
that is as far as I see,

but twig, grass, stone,
a light silt of sand
are part of Aegina, the island,

and the island is herself, is her;
some say Hygeia is
feeding a serpent from a cup,

small, intimate, not so august
as the Athenian Parthenos,
may Athené Hygeia be our near,

personal patroness;
I scrape a small pine-cone
from the sparse sea-grass

that shows separate salt-spikes
in the dry sand-drift,
I need not turn my head

to assure myself of the sea-ledge,
it is indented like a shell;
I know this, since I came here

before everything was over,
and before I realized an intimacy
near as the air.

I breathe the aloes, the acacia
of your senses, tropic red spike,
trumpet flowers, indigo petal-drift

of your remembrance,
and in your *promesse d'îles*,
there was perhaps

no such place as this,
which through antithesis,
may share super-abundance,

your phosphorescent inter-play
of gold-flecked or of rainbow-fish,
draws me to the weedy inlet

of my own *promesse*,
and a rock stark as this,
and only small crabs

and a crab-net;
sea-lavender — coriander?
no, these are camomile-daisies

that I crush as I reach out;
Arabian-gum fragrance?
no, that was the amber-beads

on the cherry-bark,
and the sticky pine-bark,
and sassafras-bark that we bit on,

and some dusty butter-and-eggs
(wild snap-dragon)
in a hot lane;

these are not here,
but I cherish my personal treasures,
now that I discover

how different yours are;
we meet in antitheses;
no need to speak, to heed one another.

That's it, I can sit here
on my rock-throne,
not moving,

or moving with everything,
like Cassiopea on her star-chair,
moving round the pole,

moving with the whole,
part of your giant-concept
of deserts, the earth entire

with water-fronts, sea-slopes,
storm, wind and thunder-crash;
I am perfectly supple and silent,

as I steal out (still lying here)
and integrate with the fan-weed,
the bubble-weed and the strings and straggle

of the long under-sea grass;
I do not compete with your vast concept,
the prick of pine-needles brings me back,

yet I am a part of it
as I am part of the spiked
or smooth or lacquered sea-grass.

But O, it goes further than that,
further than that;
as I am swept away

in the orgy of your poetry,
to tents, *térébinthe*, the hot sand
(you are not dead in the darkness),

and you draw me out
to compete with your frenzy;
there are other roses,

l'odeur solennelle des roses,
though the five-petalled *rose sauvage*
(pentagram of the alchemists)

sustains me, and the laurel
or the olive of our *grove of academe*,
yet your words free me,

I am alive in your recognition;
Athené stands guardian,
and there is ecstasy and healing

in her acceptance of the ποιητής fantasy,
her serpent feeding
from a cup . . .

O, Lady, ineffable favour,
you sent him here,
or did he glide down

of his own will and endeavour?
I touch his head and his throat
where your hands have fondled him,

my hands run along his proud length,
filled with milk from your cup
and honey from your rocks;

surely he speaks to me,
toute parfumée — your *mélisse?*
it is you he incorporates,

and his speech is the poet's speech,
j'aviverai du sel
les bouches mortes du désir.

Were you born in a palm-swamp?
how did you get here?
they say Aphaia

is goddess of the Aegina temple;
they tell us that Aphaia
(god or goddess?) was akin

to the Cretan Artemis;
Cretan Artemis? they must mean
the snake-goddess;

in Athens, Athené conquers the serpent
coiled at her heel;
here, he is intimate, I think,

her familiar, like the owl;
she is nearer Egypt
and the asp or uraeus'

head-dress of initiates;
here, in my head, you are,
speaking words,

indited on parchment,
not always easy to decipher,
but pertinent to us, here to-day,

as well as to *les sables aux limites du monde*;
you give us authentic prayer,
ouvre ma bouche dans la lumière.

But here, I don't know what you mean,
does anyone? what are you
lois de transhumance et de derivation?

are we translated, transubstantiated,
derived from tree and fish?
rest under my branches,

believe me, I would be
your *hybride très rare*
de rosier-ronce hymalayen;

you would not recognize me,
as all fretful traces of humanity
vanished; from under my thorn and leaf,

you would be wrapt away
into your own charted sky,
no one else knows the way;

you would meet the Gorgon, the Monster again,
slay, and accept Fate,
(*que ce monde est insane*),

lost — lost — lost —
what is *Exil* but a gift's bestowal,
the goddess' recompense?

But it can't be, it can't be,
it is you who are *très rare* and far,
at one with Time and the star-cycle;

by antitheses, I become ant or eel,
nothingness slides off this rock;
growing in perceptiveness,

I become small snake,
not quite invisible, inhuman, (*transhumance?*)
I am conscious of my exquisite spine

(God's work) as I slip and swing;
no bird could be swifter in air,
no gull, hawk or lark could be happier;

go Perseus, man and hero,
your perfection permits this,
it is your gift, my mind's opposite;

leaving it all, leaving the *île de promesse*,
I float, swim and dart now,
straight to the antithetical centre.

You will understand,
perhaps one or two others will understand,
no one else, the aim, the pursuit

(is he dead in the darkness?) of this other
of whom your *transhumance* wrought miracle,
miracle out of majic,

his eyes' amber; your *derivation*,
whatever you meant by that,
transformed my self-seeking

quest to content;
I could rest anyhow;
I need not quibble over why or where,

or why did he come at all,
or why didn't he come sooner;
now, a snake in the wood,

now a snake in the shallows,
now green, blue and vermillion vanish
in deep water; I am only movement and colour,

but God, give me back my thousand exquisite
jointed bones, my spine's rapture
(your work) I would go further.

Where, where, where, do I go?
I know the way, but my step is uncertain,
if I gain humanity again;

I can not cling indecently to your aloes,
your palm-trees, or can I?
is physical weakness indecent?

it seems so when I think of Bar-Isis,
that Memnon in the desert;
were his words ironical?

"You look well," he said,
and those were his last words,
when I saw him in a strange place

with others there; he would write, he said,
and he did and I answered and waited for another letter,
but apparently, it was over;

he was not quite 40,
I was over 70, so I read you again;
I would recall your Istar, Baal or another,

and let humanity go;
arrogant, impudent, I won't stop,
I won't look under me;

the unfathomable belongs to you,
sand, dune, heap and mound,
continent, empire; I passed winged fish

and stark meteors of fish-shoals;
I need never speak, I am as unimportant to them there
as I was in the upper air;

Aegina begot me, yes,
you and the *Grove* are there,
but ultimately I must track down this Asmodel,

Paris, Bar-Isis; I must creep into his cavern,
beat my hand on his breast,
wake his heart to this instant . . .

I say, I don't know what he thinks,
I say, I don't care,
but that isn't true either,

but was it quite fair of fate
to accost me with amber,
Egyptian eyes' amber

in an ordinary man's face?
I can't stop and wonder,
inventing a problematical reaction,

what he might think, say, answer
to my *Notre Dame* revelation,
the *Astrologie, Alchimie, Magie*

of the three doors,
one can't hurl such findings
in the face of a stranger,

anyhow, it was over,
I stopped waiting for a letter,
and into the veil rent,

as through parted curtains
was the exact intellectual component
or the exact emotional opposite,

your cool laurel, the olive silver-green,
to compensate or off-set the reddest rose,
this enigmatic encounter.

How wonderful to strike my breast
and cry "I have sinned, I have sinned,"
but you, *Seigneur*, won't permit this;

darting straight like fire,
I remember your Baal, your Istar,
my bones remember;

where am I going?
you named Memnon,
he sang, did he, in the sun,

the first sun-ray . . . swift, swift,
be swift to come, the first of a million,
of the million-million sun-rays,

one must strike first,
let me be that one;
now there is one note;

out of the sea, over the sand,
a symbol, obelisk, no man,
Memnon, Bar-Isis, son of Dawn.

Mais Dieu se tait dans le quantième —
what do you mean,
what do you mean, *Seigneur?*

is there an inch in the square,
or a million-million miles,
its equivalent in the outer sphere,

where God keeps quiet?
but I am not God,
this is a nervous invective,

I haven't got there to your *quantième*,
which I read *quatrième*
but I don't understand, anyway.

Seigneur, it is no good,
your perfection carried me along,
but it's gone; not your incomparable challenge

to time — time — time —
your sequence of invocations,
your magnificent rhythms;

you showed me how I could cling
to a Greek rock and how I could slide away,
but did you show me how I could come back

to ordinary time-sequence,
neither insect, reptile
nor illimitable sun-ray?

I want my old habit,
I want to light candles;
Seigneur, you must forgive my deflection,

I can not step over the horizon;
I must wait to-day, to-morrow or the day after
for the answer.

PART THREE

Star of Day

(January 24 – February 19, 1961)

[1]

So at last I find Asmodel,
the second of the *génies zodiacaux,*
to whom one may cry,

exhaussez mon incantation, ma prière . . .
raise up, lift up, receive my recognition,
and this at last, with no reservation,

right, left?
win, lose?
for you are dead;

they say, Saïs brought forth the Star of Day,
at midnight when the shadows are most dense,
the nights longest and most desperate,

it was Plutarch spoke of Saïs . . .
we know the rest,
Isis, Cybele (Atys), *Notre Dame;*

was Saïs a capital of upper Egypt,
on the Delta? I don't know,
at any rate, Saïs, what have you done?

what has the word done?
you include but in small grandeur,
the whole circle of the sun.

So it was in the winter,
it was in the depth of night,
just as my Christmas candles had burnt out,

that you were born
into a new cycle,
one of the zodiac angels,

one of the countless others,
yet remaining yourself,
integrated with the Star of Day;

night here; I am fearful and timid,
taking a stumbling way
toward you, failing in fortitude,

turning back to the incantation I wrote,
I need no rosary
of sesame,

only the days' trial,
reality . . .
remembering

how then, I was waiting
for a letter
that never came;

I wrote the *rosary*
in September,
you were on the way;

it was six months
since that first meeting,
and a little over nine months to the day,

late winter (it was very dark,
just as my Christmas candles
had burnt out),

that you were born,
(you had died, they said),
integrated with the Star of Day.

It was April that we met,
and once in May;
I did not realize my state of mind,

my "condition" you might say,
until August when I wrote,
the reddest rose unfolds,

I did not realize that separation
was the only solution,
if I were to resolve this curious "condition,"

you were five months "on the way,"
I did not realize how intimate
the relation, nor what lay ahead;

I did know that I must keep faith
with something, I called it writing,
write, write or die,

the rose, the fire, the flame
must be maintained — but how?
it was Venice-Venus (Isis)

génerateur, générant,
never to be gainsaid,
who ordered, ordained or controlled this,

and compelled my stylus, pen or pencil
as I wrote, *I walk into you,*
Doge — Venice —

I did not think of it the other way,
that it was you who walked into me,
the experience was unprecedented,

a fire eating me up,
but a fire to be sustained,
anyhow, now it was too late

to reject fate,
you were nearer than you ever were,
you are my whole estate.

Then I turned to another,
formal and external,
who had found the way,

it was necessary to keep contact
with intellect and achievement
to balance *the last desperate non-escape,*

with *transhumance* and *derivation,*
to be swept in a whirlwind,
to far *îles de promesse,*

not mine but another's;
but I must return to my own nun-grey;
I didn't know why

I must recover the human equation,
until I turned over these pages,
and read *I want to light candles,*

true, Christmas was on the way,
and the angel Azrael,
not of death but of birth.

I said, "Azrael said,
'you spoke of Asmodel,
as if in reproval,'"

no wonder, his hand was on your shoulder,
I was in the way,
I was no partner

to that fellowship,
I had had my day,
but I didn't know that;

I didn't know you had fallen into a trap,
the reddest rose;
renouncement? feu d'enfer?

it was September, three months to go,
but I didn't know that; anyway,
it was too late to cast you out.

Rain falls or snow, I don't know,
only I must stumble along, grope along,
find my way; but believe me,

I have much to sustain me,
though for the moment, dim with inanition,
I don't conjure you,

name your name, I don't try to,
but at least, I found Asmodel,
the second in the zodiac circle,

and I can if I want to, pray
exhaussez mon incantation, ma prière . . .
but what do I pray?

"let him forget, let him forget the past,
let him wander with the shade or substance
of the one he loved best on earth?"

no, I don't pray that;
what do I pray really?
"separate us now eternally,

let severance be complete,
the cord is cut?" no;
I have nine months to remember.

. . . only an end to the whole adventure,
it stops here,
I wrote in *Academe,*

but it had to go on the full time,
an emotional seizure?
ecstasy? fantasy? insanity?

no matter, it brought me back to the room
where we had first talked together,
it was informal and friendly,

only when I had no letter,
I felt cast out, I was thrown away,
and to recover identity,

I wrote furiously,
I was in a fever, you were lost,
just as I had found you,

but I went on, I had to go on,
the writing was the un-born,
the conception.

Now you are born
and it's all over,
will you leave me alone?

whether you have gone to archangels and lovers
or to infernal adventures,
I don't know,

I only know,
this room contains me,
it is enough for me,

there is always an end;
now I draw my nun-grey about me
and know adequately,

the reddest rose,
the unalterable law . . .
Night brings the Day.

SAGESSE

(Summer – Winter 1957)

You look at me, a hut or cage contains
your fantasy, your frantic stare;

"a white-faced Scops owl from Sierra Leone,
West Africa," I read, under a picture in *The Listener,*

and this is Whitsun, June the ninth, and I must find
the Angel or the Power that rules this hour;

I find the name *Aneb*, with the attribute,
Dieu clément for the hour, and for the day,

Dieu propice with the name *Siré*;
Viroaso is the angel for the day, and for the hour,

we may invoke the angel, *Thopitus*;
do these rebuke me? what can I do, my friend?

I can only say, "O white-faced Scops,
stare out, glare out, live on . . ."

May those who file before you feel
something of what you are — that God is kept within

the narrow confines of a cage, a pen;
they will laugh and linger and some child may shudder,

touched by the majesty, the lifted wings,
the white mask and the eyes that seem to see,

like God, everything and like God, see nothing;
our small impertinence, our little worth

is invisible in the day; when darkness comes,
you will be no more a fool, a clown,

a white-faced Scops, a captive and in prison,
but noble and priest and soldier, scribe and king

will hail you, sacrosanct, while frail women
bend and sway between the temple pillars,

till the torches flicker and fail,
and there is only faint light from the braziers

and the ghostly trail of incense, and cries of recognition
and of gladness in the fragrant air.

"O, look, he's comical, his baggy trousers
and his spindly legs — you've still got half a bun";

"he won't eat buns," the father says,
"but mice and such, look at his claws,

a vampire — yes, he's comical, look at his nose
and whiskers — proper make-up for a Guy";

the child remembers something, draws away,
she thinks, "I never saw a farthing,

it's half a ha'pence, but she said, teacher or somebody,
or Mr. Spence, that there were two, not owls,

some other birds, sold for a farthing — and what else?"
He said, "*without your Father, no bird falls*,"

I don't know where or what it's all about;
I wish I could go home, get out of here;

he must be angry if he liked the birds;
I wish they wouldn't laugh, it isn't funny,

and this one's bigger than — than a hundred others,
sparrows, I think it was.

An owl hooted out in the darkness,
so the angel came — what angel and what name?

is it Tara, *Dieu fontaine de sagesse*
and the angel Ptébiou? it was his hour

or near his hour, what did he say?
a caller before noon, had spoken of owls here,

"*Uhu*," she said, "*great owl, Waldkauz, the wood-owl*,"
and she translated *Kauz* as a queer fellow;

I showed the picture and she said, "how beautiful";
how strange, how wonderful, that last night

was the first night that it came,
the distant summons, the muted cry, the call,

and my bones melted and my heart was flame,
and all I wished was freedom and to follow

the voice, not very far, not very near,
a voice that changed our lake, the *Zürisee*,

into a mystery, the haunted mere of *Märchen*
and old legends, or even Lethe or Eunoë, now and here.

Without your Father, without your Father —
what does that mean? my father's talking to the gardener

or the man who sweeps the papers — "yes, they're pretty,
      mum,
the deers" — does it mean animals? does He run, too,

on little hooves like that one, does He jump
and stand (now) like that biggest one with horns,

straight up against the wire? he's looking over;
I wish I'd kept my half-bun,

not crumbed it for the pelicans — birds, too?
I'd like to feel his tongue upon my hand;

that boy is frightened — "let me help" — "he'll bite —"
"you can't reach up" — "O yes, O yes, I can,

he's looking at us" — "stand on the keeper's box,
he's busy talking" — "but, but, you take it,

it's your piece of bun —" "no fear, you're welcome, miss —
but your dad's come"— my father? my father?

but this deer is my father — "a funny kid,
it's my fault, mister" — "now, you hop down" —

"yes, yes, I'm coming" — but I'm somewhere else,
he kissed my hand, we're somewhere in the forest . . .

I never thanked the boy, was he God, too . . .

Goot — Goed — *Dieu qui reçoit les pécheurs*
and *Dieu qui rejouit*, the angel, Ptéchout

and the angel, Aterchinis, and Sister Annie brings my
    coffee,
and I say, "how are you?" and she says, "gut — gut";

Goot and Goed, Scotch and Belgium, my book says,
Goot, gut and good and surely God, and so we play

this game of affirmations and of angels' names,
this Sunday, one week after Whitsun;

though I can not say Ptéchout and I must look again
to see if Aterchinis is spelt right, Goot, Goed seems easy

and the way direct; "gut — gut," I'll say and Goot will
    surely answer;
God who receives sinners? what are we?

and Goed is "gut," actually some say "goed" here,
some of the simple people, they are sinless,

we have known the desperate day of Cain,
none of us blameless, but a proud angel says,

"I serve Him who receives the outcast," and another says,
"I bring happiness and serve God who rejoices."

And there is Good, just good, *anglaise,*
la droite de Dieu, Syth is the angel,

and where are we now? seven weeks after Whitsun,
since to-day is August 4th; the owl day was June 9th,

and Good, just good, is June the 21st,
and the other days for Good, are April 10,

September 1, November 12, January 23,
so we find round the year-dial, each God-attribute,

five times, each flame, each angel's name
that corresponds again to hours and minutes;

but it is simple, Good, anyone can understand,
Good — *anglaise* — not anyone, it is profound and subtle,

for my room is fragrant with enchantment,
with the flowers he left, and I am taken far away

by Goth, Gott, *Germain,*
the Sun, *Dieu admirable.*

He went away, Goth, the German, *Germain,*
degrees, days, hours, minutes,

how many? he left the flowers, August the 3rd,
this is October 17th and they say,

he comes back in three days — will he?
who will come back? a wandering flame,

a name, Goth, Gott, *Dieu admirable,* or another?
what Sun will rise, what darkness will unclose?

what spark, diastole, systole, compel, repel?
what counter-appeal contract the heart?

or not, what mystery? shall the winter-branch
be broken, fuel for another? or shall the branch,

prouder than spring, lordlier than summer,
strike deeper and grow higher to disclose

the last enchantment,
the white winter-rose?

Germain said, "isn't it over-weighted?
can you have so many angels' names,

a list of dates, months, days,
a prose in-set? or is it poetry? Egypt,

hieratic rhythm, then the most ordinary association,"
but I said, "isn't that the whole point, anyway?"

what am I doing? am I swept into a cycle
of majestic Spirits, myself aspiring yet questioning

my right to mention even one of the seventy-two regents
of the great Temple of the *Œdipus Ægyptiacus*?

am I in some way, culpable? or does the magnetic sway
of the vast cycle require this space, this place,

this corner of this room, to prove the might
of the infinitely great to protect

the most minute, the almost invisible spark, from the
    extraneous chaos,
the impenetrable outer gloom?

Or is it a great tide that covers the rock-pool
so that it and the rock are indistinguishable

from the sea-shelf and are part of the sea-floor,
though the sea-anemone may quiver apprehensively

and the dried weed uncurl painfully
and the salt-sediment rebel, "I was salt,

a substance, concentrated, self-contained,
am I to be dissolved and lost?"

"it is fearful, I was a mirror, an individual,"
cries the shallow rock-pool, "now infinity

claims me; I am everything? but nothing";
peace, salt, you were never as useful as all that,

peace, flower, you are one of a thousand-thousand others,
peace, shallow pool, be lost.

His is the 24th decade of the sphere,
his is the angel Senciner, the time of invocation

or of prayer is 3.40 until 4 — what do we do?
we clear the table, pile books on a chair,

slide out of boudoir-slippers, grope anxiously for shoes,
open a window to the winter-air, close it again,

run a comb through our hair; Germain is critical;
why should we care? we must present another self, a shell,

we are too tense, too brittle; fearfully we pray for strength,
O Senciner, you who watched our Œdipus, our father,

let us endure, let us forget anxiety and terror
for a brief fraction of your decade of the sphere.

Regent of distant fire and snow
and what is near, Senciner,

the Temple of our father, *Œdipus Ægyptiacus*,
the shadow of the portal on the sand, the lintel

and the painted walls, where any child may read
our fate in images of birds and bees,

while the scribe, the initiate and the desperate wait,
faltering before the threshold,

blinded by the Sun; where are we?
how do we meet here? where have you gone?

but this is Germain, fearing my abstraction,
"why are you trembling?

what are you thinking?
I don't know where you are;

you must come out, the car will come to-morrow,
you haven't been out for a week;

you loved the trees, like brides, you said,
verzaubert, you loved you said, the forest,

geisterhaft im Nebel, the *Nebelzauberwald;*
is five o'clock too late?"

Sotis, Sothis, Sith, Venus, Venus, Mercury, be near,
these Regents rule these planets and these planets serve

to mark the decants, to concentrate, control
the actual space reserved for *Dieu qui exauce les pécheurs,*

Dieu rédempteur and *Dieu seul et unique*;
their hour is six to seven, carelessly we sleep,

or wake to fear the peril of another day,
while Venus, Venus, Mercury despair,

yet still this Trinity sends out its message
through the winter-dark, "arise, arise, re-animate,

O Spirit, this small ark, this little body,
this small separate self; of the world's mortals,

make but one immortal, let but one awake,
to set the dead pyre flaming,

that the Phoenix, Venus, Venus, Mercury
may fire the world with ecstasy,

with Love who forgets our faults,
with Love who redeems the lost,
with Love, Love, Love *unique*."

What of the other Regents of the night? Lost?
no, Germain, hold me close, peach-blossom petals fall

outside a bamboo-shelter — is it four? or five? or earlier?
what Trinity shall we call, to spread the silken covers

of our bed? here, the rain drips
and snow, just turned to rain, upon the windows,

and the window-panes are clouded with this winter-rain
     and snow;
this is our day — the night? shall we renounce

the later fruit, the peach and pomegranate,
cleft open, ripe to be taken, eaten?

your pride, your dignity, my own reticence
demands perfection; not here, where we meet

in friendly talk, "I heard a symphony, Cherubini,
new to me, yesterday when you left,

I think that he knew Liszt;
funny, you were quite right,

Purcell is much, much earlier than Mozart;
to-morrow, then?" he bows and on my hand

peach-blossom petals fall,
this is the day, the one kiss that we know.

71

We should keep vigil, wait alert
till Venus "strikes," the day is full of petty cares

and other people's woes and pain, and rain, always
    the rain,
and little joys and the great joy, Germain;

she comes at night, from Egypt, Seket,
while we sleep, 1.20 to be exact,

and at 6 and at 6.20, as we wrote, Sotis and Sothis;
then she comes again, mid-morning from the Hesperides,

at 10.40, can the day be dark?
wait for her at 3.20 and at 8;

what right have we to fear frustration and incompetence?
our share of bliss is infinite,

the angels' names are symphonies;
how can we fret

and wear our nerves to shreds,
knowing the clock will "strike,"

the rose and the camellia spread their flame,
when the early flowering of the peach is over.

From Egypt first, how dark, how dark the night,
myself a mound of earth, shivering but inert,

and Germain says, "your weakness and your nerves
are due to apprehension; if you write like this, create,

you must expect reaction"; "but this is different,"
I say, "I know the symptoms, as you seem to call them,

but nothing like this happened when I wrote before";
"are these poems more intense? I do not know,

I can not follow your degrees and angels";
does he know what he is? I do not know,

but *Dieu sauveur* last night was manifest,
the attribute of Seket and her hour,

1.20 while we sleep;
no infant in the straw,

but simply Mary's flower,
"Marah" the *Grande Mer*, patron and protectress,

sword-lilies on their stalks,
Créatrice de la Foi . . .

As Mary bowed before her Son, so I bow down,
not to Germain, but in a way, to you, Germain;

"german," the near-relation, "german," first;
but that awaits the flower,

seed that creates the fruit;
"you should be happy that I'm tired and worn,

giving my life-force to these little songs,
instead of carping at me" — "what is carping?"

"O, grumbling, scolding, urging this or that,
I can not take a trip to Sicily,

or even to Lugano, and talk of this is torture,
for you know, I can't go there,

I can't go anywhere, but you can go,
O, Germain, go, go, go — I've yet to chart my way

to the mysterious Melindais or the Zaflanians,
or even find again

the Regents and the Decants that I know,
Illyrian or Bohemian . . ."

Sombre Mère Sterile and *Brillante Mère Féconde,*
the light and dark; you hold the planets steady

in their course, you and your Son,
and there is no land where you are not found,

no hour, when you are not near,
and you are always here,

to spread the picture-book upon my bed,
to show me who you are, Tara, Miri, Mara,

with mountain-cherries like the mountain-snow,
or golden weed washed up on golden sand,

with shells like small rose-whorls,
and shells like hollow bowls,

and the one special shell you choose for me,
among the myriad-myriad others;

this is my shell, you hold it to my ear,
"listen, my child, fear not the ancient lore,

(*Gymnosophes, Philosophes*), this echo is for you,
listen, my child, it is enough,

the echo of the sea, our secret
and our simple mystery, *Grande Mer* . . ."

A thread, a strand, 72 angels' names . . .
how to go on? we have named 7 of these;

the seventh is Senciner, and then, three more,
and then another, Seket and her hour;

O mother-father, Seket-Senciner, at the end, we found
a bowl, a shell, at first, an owl, a deer,

that's how it started, the child compassed it,
began and closed the circle . . .

"now mum's fanciful," she thinks;
we're sitting in our kitchen, here in London,

"duckie, just put the kettle on," mum says,
if only she'd forget that day, last summer,

"you did come over queer," she says,
"what was the matter? four places, ducks,

Uncle Alf's coming in — brr, winter —
real pea-soup outside, yes, draw the curtains,

nice, turkey-red, I always says,
I'm thinking of that screech-owl

and those deer — my, it was hot that day,
do you remember?"

"It was twenty thousand, just in London,
funny, we're here . . . that was the big Blitz,

there was more come after . . .
those buzz-bombs and the chandeliers —"

"come, come, Alf, a cup of tea is what you want,
don't go on thinking of it — dad said he might be late —

that was long over"; "I wake up in the night
and think, by Christ, it never was

or it was somewhere else or I was somewhere else,
Gawd only knows — "don't swear so, Alf —"

"Swearing? how I could curse,
if duckie didn't look at me, like that —"

"O, ducks all right — go open for your dad,
that was his knock . . .

how often must I tell you, Alf,
that our ducks sees too much and hears too much,

and calls out in the night,
maybe, she isn't bright or maybe, she's too bright,

praying-like or singing-like, I wouldn't know;
she screams or sings, *Father, Father,*

then I shake her up and wake her up
and call to Bert, and say,

'duckie, what is it dear?
what is it now? dad's here.'"

"The Slaughter of the Innocents, that's what it was;
I never look at ducks and her white face,

but what I see —" "O, Alf, shut up,
we can't go back —" "— for you and me,

and tough blokes like me and Bert,
perhaps, it was coming to us,

but for such as she —" "they're coming, hush—"
"— she'll help her dad off with his coat,

grown-up and proper, ask of the shop,
talks like a little lady, formal,

she'll take his scarf and lay it on the rack,
like she done just now for me — I never see —"

"Alf, Alf, you'll drive me crazy —"
"O, I'm proper sorry, after all you done —"

"What did I do?" "O, you and such as you,
you kept us all going, kept the world,

if you get my meaning, on its feet,
you going out blitz nights for lost cats —

O you can laugh, and we laughed then, by golly,
you with the Blue Cross pinned on your old coat."

Someone said, "poor little tyke,"
and a man from dad's shop who talks funny,

said "*Christkind*," and mum said "hush" at him,
and said to me, "that's German for a good girl,

are you a good girl, duckie?"
I stack the dishes and I wring the dish-cloth,

like mum says; I clean the sink with Rinso,
not too much; I shake the mat before the door,

I water the geranium — is this being good?
mum says, "good girl"; I do this not for mum

or anyone; I do it for myself; if I go on,
I make a sort of track, I can't say what,

it's pebbles and hard stones, it's something in a story,
I can't say where it goes —

it goes from where I brush the carpet on the stair,
to the landing just above.

Mum said I was took queer,
I don't know what I said,

I know I'll never say it any more,
only to myself, I say it over and over,

when I'm in bed . . .

———————

Let the child sleep, let the world sleep,
few can endure Teut, Agad, Hana, Sila,

the names you share with God,
Grande Mer . . . few can endure

the ecstasy, the fever,
the folding and unfolding of a flower;

can I endure your beauty and your favour?
the day moves on and you were here at dawn,

Sotis and Sothis; the day moves on toward dark,
I wait the after mid-night Messenger,

all day I wait for her, Seket from Egypt,
with the red Egyptian lily in her hand.

Lady of chaste hands and the quiet mind,
we have neglected you, being faint and numb,

inert, resentful, at 10.40, of the day,
looking backward to the night that's past,

looking forward to the night to come;
Ouestucati, your decant brings the sea-wind

and the level plain of *Leuké*, that white sand;
you come from the Hesperides,

how can we greet you here?
how can we meet you there?

O chaste, immaculate, accept our feeble effort,
our faint prayer; in you, there is no conflict

with the hours, the seasons and the minutes;
we would bear a flickering taper to you,

O most fair; unworthy, we would pray
your intercession for us; grant us strength,

a little strength to serve your Power,
O *Leuké*-lily of this morning hour.

At 3.20, we served you meanly, Siêmé;
true, we awaited Senciner at 3.40,

who would carry us on till 4, and of this Trinity,
we did not note your predecessor, Tépiseuth, at 3;

(*could you not watch with me one hour*)
but now the flowers of every season,

brighten and unfold, Germain is here . . .
dive deep, dive deep, dive deeper,

for the 4 and 5 await you, through and under
the other side of the sphere,

and all the other numbers in their order;
at 3.20, we served you meanly, Siêmé,

but still the Sotis, Sothis radiance of the dawn
followed us, and still the brilliance

of the after-midnight Seket tracked us down,
and still the morning Leuké held her own;

at 3.20, we served you meanly, Siêmé,
but now to-day, all day, all days forever,

daignez m'éclairer, me garder, me dirigez,
Ange du Seigneur.

Dans le Soleil, il a placé sa tente,
et c'est Lui-même qui s'avance,

comme un Epoux hors de la couche nuptiale,
so Time and the Sun move on to the *Béthuliens,*

when Venus "strikes" at 8;
I don't know who they are or where,

but laugh, they say, laugh, laugh, like children . . .
laugh, they say, like simpletons, like idiots,

fools and poets; laugh the world away,
laugh, laugh and place your flowers

on the shrine of Teut, Agad, Hana, Sila
who share your name, *Soleil.*

WINTER LOVE

(Espérance)

(January 3 – April 15, 1959)

                  . . . ten years?
it was more than that, more than that;
your hand grips mine — masterless?

I was masterless while men fought,
and I only found Spirit to match my Spirit,
when I met Achilles in a trance, a dream,

a life out-lived,
another life re-lived,
till I came back, came back . . .

If I thought of you, I only thought
of something that endured, that might endure;
I did not know of Circe and her power,

I had not even heard Calypso named, nor Nausicaä,
Penelope was a far-off dream of home,
and others and the quarrel in the tents

(fight for Criseus, war for Briseus)
was only a local matter, far below
the turrets and the ramparts and the Wall;

I loved Achilles finally, in *Leuké*,
but I let him go, back to the sea,
back to his mother, Thetis;

so he was absorbed, re-claimed by his own element?
I do not know, Odysseus — your name is unfamiliar;
I had not thought of it nor spoken it,

for ten years — it is more than ten years;
then, you were in and out as they all were at the Palace,
it is more, more than ten years . . .

Now there is winter-love, a winter-lover
who would take gladly — fondling the crisp leaves
with a padded paw, sheathed — glad to find

in the den, the sacred lair, no trap to entice,
no rapacious loins, and sighs, not groans —
no rain of arrows, no poisonous thrust of spears,

no thundering on the stairs,
no rasp of steel,
only Taygetus' silence,

till a drift of snow
slides from a branch,
then, silence more intense.

Why break the spell?
why name the mountain Ida?
true, Paris, *Idaean Paris* was most dear,

and he was slain and rose and found —
was it Oenone? did he find her again?
don't speak of Paris lest I goad you on

with other names, enchantments, Circe —
would you have Circe now?
they were there in a fever, Circe, Calypso —

but I did not remember, I did not remember —
true, there were others and you were ruthless
and too familiar — you married your Princess,

but afterwards, you left Ithaca for another, *Helen,*
Fate, Fortune, Defamation,
Treachery, Adultery, War.

So we were together
though I did not think of you
for ten years;

it is more than ten years
and the long time after;
I was with you in Calypso's cave?

no, no — I had never heard of her,
but I remember the curve of honey-flower
on an old wall, I recall

the honey-flower as I saw it
or seemed to see it
for the first time,

its horn was longer, whiter —
what do I mean?
"bite clear the stem

and suck the honey out,"
a child companion or old grandam
taught me to suck honey

from the honey-flower;
what is Calypso's cave?
that is your grotto, your adventure;

how could I love again, ever?
repetition, repetition, Achilles, Paris, Menelaus?
but you are right, you are right,

there is something left over,
the first unsatisfied desire —
the first time, that first kiss,

the rough stones of a wall,
the fragrance of honey-flowers, the bees,
and how I would have fallen but for a voice,

calling through the brambles
and tangle of bay-berry
and rough broom,

Helen, Helen, come home;
there was a Helen before there was a War,
but who remembers her?

The-tis — Sea-'tis, I played games like this;
I had long reveries, invoked the future,
re-invoked the past, syllables, mysteries, numbers;

I must have turned a secret key, unwittingly,
when I said Odysseus — when did I say Odysseus?
how did I call you back, or how did I come back?

memory has its own strange Circe-magic,
and forgetting, stranger; forgetting utterly, I dropped
a screen, a shutter; a heavy door clanged

between Helen-Helen; "they have gone,"
"where have they gone?" "down to the Sea,
to send Odysseus off —" "*Odysseus* —"

"he was only waiting for his Ship,
a special Ship, ancestral,
the prow is painted with the ancient Eyes."

I was to meet you, I was to meet you
under the oleanders,
I was to meet you again;

"a special Ship, for festival," they said,
so Helen stared, a Maiden, still a Maiden,
though last night, escaped the grandam,

Helen was conceived under the oleanders,
that is, Helen, the future Helen
that wrecked citadels, was born.

Chorus Strophe

Heavy the hand of Fate,
heavy the chains, the bonds,
heavy, heavy, the weight of Destiny,
and there is no escape
from pre-destined torture and agony;
ground under the stones of Troy,
we are dust for eternity,
crushed by the fallen Walls,
we are helpless and none may help;
what lives and what is left
when rain levels the Trojan plain
and snow fills in the crevasses
where the Wheels of the chariots passed?
what is left, what is left of Troy?
heavy the hand of Fate
and what is more desolate
than the breach in the Wall
that sears like a gaping wound —
Troy's gate was here.

ANTISTROPHE

Frail is the thread and long,
pale is the hand and fragile,
busy upon the loom,
day and night, night and day,
re-weaving with threads of gold,
cyclamen, purple and blue,
the pattern, the history,
the legend; He steps from his throne,
Phoebus, the Lord of Troy,
into the sea, night comes;
all night, all day,
the Wheel whirrs on;
dare to defy the Sun,
dare to desecrate Beauty,
dare to say Troy is forgotten —
the Song and the Singer are one.

STROPHE

What song is left to sing?
all song is sung,
Furies clang dissonance
with iron wings;
the air blights the open rose,
the fetid air brings
death to the open field,
death to the closed
walled-in fruit garden
where the branch-in-flower clings
to the dank wall,
but de-flowered;
the discoloured flowers fall
on the path, now grown over
with poisonous weeds;
the deadly seeds of mandragora
were sown long ago.

ANTISTROPHE

Heed not the dissonance,
heed not the hiss of Death,
Helen, immaculate one,
in a maiden-dress;
your sandal is caught
in the tangle of grass,
your shoulder-clasp undone,
your tunic unloosed,
your small breast swells
ripening under the kiss
of the ravening Hero.

O, Helen, most blest,
O, *Virgo*, unravaged,
but knowing the thirst
of the moment un-mated;
the insatiable thirst
will lead to Achilles,
the forest of masts,
that moment unsatisfied,
will brighten the earth
with the myth and the legend,
the exquisite breath
of almond and apple, quince-flower,
the pomegranate flower-cup . . .
O, Helen, most blest,
recall first love and last.

Helen's breasts, it was always Helen's breasts,
and the wine-cup that they wrought,
called Helen's breast;

cover my shoulder
for the wind howls louder,
outside this hunting-lodge,

perched on Taygetus' cliff;
O, I was ready to leave Sparta,
a second time — O, I was ready enough

to escape — to follow you,
and we will not starve;
you say there is dried fruit

in the amphora and the wine-jars,
but I would wander in the Elysian-fields
and find the Tree for myself — for myself —

with a special low down-sweeping burdened bough,
low enough so that I could kneel
and savour the fragrance of the cleft fruit

on the branch, intoxicant;
I would be intoxicated with the scent of fruit,
O, holy apple, O, ripe ecstasy . . .

but believe me, believe me
I am grateful
that you came for me,

I am content,
besieged with memories,
like low-swarming bees.

Every bone aches with the cold,
but I was glad to come,
glad to come with you here;

in my old hunting-cloak and hunting-boots,
I felt young as we plunged into the drift,
leaving that hateful palace

and the trophies and the tedious tales,
told over and over at the endless banquets;
I was waiting for something,

though I did not know what,
till you burst upon us,
with tangled hair and beard,

and salt-streaked seaman's cloak
and the old secret sly, wily undaunted look
that recalled me — and I remembered

how you fondled my breast, and the moment
of fulfilment was broken by a voice,
Helen come home, and I went back;

I expected to know more, expected completion,
but they said, "he has gone,
he was only waiting for his Ship."

Comfort me, then, Odysseus, King of Men,
but do not turn, the cold seeps through
the fleeces and the furs; the pelts lie heavy on me

but I dare not move; this is reality;
I choose the spell, or enchantment,
stronger than my poor will, bore Helen far,

and then Achilles' eyes turned to the Sea,
and then I felt that Paris yearned
for his first love, Oenone,

and I was left to vanish like a ghost,
or seek the stony path, return,
the thorns, reality;

a wish, a whim and Menelaus came;
Theseus had long since found the gods,
for Theseus, Olympos — but I knew no god
    but perseverance;

endure, endurance was to be my Saviour,
but why endure when Love closes the door
and one is left, locked in an empty fortress,

a soulless Palace, soulless till you came,
and there was yet another world to conquer,
or space or time, reality of a steep climb,

a mountain-path,
remembrance of narcissus-buds to come,
buried now, under the snow.

Half-hibernating under the pelts and furs,
till you break free, break away, replenish the fire,
count and re-count the wine-jars,

"there is one," I thought, "stuffed with dried fruit,
perhaps a trick to disguise, to hide
this exquisite Samian,"

Samos? Samian? it is not so cold,
and Odysseus tears the thick furs from the couch
to make mats and a rug to the fire-place,

and light dances on the walls,
hung with rich tapestries, it seems,
though they are only bear-pelts and wild-panther,

and the fire sings, and "there are more candles,
hidden in this oat-bin," he says;
who had ridden here?

who had prepared the lodge for future visits?
who had hidden candles,
and sealed the precious Samos

in an unpainted jar
to hide it from the others?
what Love, what Lovers' tryst?

Who has been here before?
was it Iacchus, Dionysus, Bacchus?
fragrance of grapes mingles with scent of cedar

and apple-wood; though we have only fir-wood and dried
    cones,
altar-incense — and the hiss of resin

recalls a whisper or the echo of a whisper
in a temple-corridor — we are not alone.
Helen was lost, she sought reality,

let go the dream; Achilles sought the Sea,
and Paris found his earlier love, Oenone;
true, true, but life returns, we have not far to go,

when Love kindles the flame;
why fear the dark without,
when light returns within?

O, do not bring snow-water
but fresh snow;
I would be bathed with stars,

new fallen from heaven,
one with the cloud,
my forehead ringed

with icy frost, a crown;
let my mind flash with blades,
let thought return,

unravel the thick skein,
woven of tangled memory and desire,
lust of the body, hunger, cold and thirst;

our hidden lair has sanctified *Virgo*,
the lost, unsatisfied, the broken tryst,
the half-attained;

love built on dreams
of the forgotten first unsatisfied embrace,
is satisfied.

STROPHE

The first kiss and the last kiss and between,
the surging armies,
the swaying masts,
the shifting scene;

wake up, wake up in *Leuké*, Helen,
that was a dream; how could earth draw you back,
Sparta, Taygetus? why should Odysseus leave

unslaked adventure, boundless horizons,
unconquered citadels for home? no Ithaca, no Sparta
could recall him to the islands,

the small world of Greece;
but you, you thought of reparation and release,
and dreamed Odysseus "true," forgetting Paris;

wake up, wake up, Helen, recall Oenone
and restore their youth; no madness, no dissonance,
but reverence of old laws, no stolen bliss;

not Paris-Helen but Oenone-Paris;
song would redress the ancient grief,
the spear-thrust, death and loss,

the first kiss and the last kiss and between,
the surging armies,
the swaying masts,
the shifting scene.

ANTISTROPHE

You dreamed of lost embraces
and Taygetus' snow — let Paris go
back to Oenone and their wooded hills,

let Achilles, like Odysseus,
with worn and battered gear
or radiant new-winged prows, sail far

to conquer undiscovered worlds
with words — "peace, peace" — or with a Holy War;
Apollo on the Walls, they say,

appeared to men as Paris;
perhaps he manifested as Achilles, too,
or even as Odysseus — who may know?

Achilles? Odysseus? Paris?
but it was from Song, you took the seed,
the sun-seed from the Sun;

none may turn back
who know that last inseminating kiss;
this is your world, *Leuké*,

reality of the white sand,
the meadow . . .
Parthenos.

STROPHE

Odysseus' fretful brow,
Achilles' cunning steel,
and Paris' apple — you have them now,

the adventure and the glory
and the seeds of fruit to sow —
how many grains of pomegranate or apple?

conjure a magic circle of fruit-trees,
with roots to hold *Leuké*, the island-Helen,
in a firm embrace,

an inescapable net,
until the flowers are full
and waft and spill fragrance, enchantment;

who can break the will
of seed to grow?
Paris-Oenone?

Helen, commend their happiness
and so invoke the greater bliss
of Helios-Helen-Eros.

ANTISTROPHE

Rise from your apathy, your dream,
the die was cast and Helen lost;
leave lovers to their happiness

and grope your way, ignoble and defenceless
in the dark; yours was the guilt;
slough off the fantasy, accept the tangible,

go out, go out, go forth,
renounce the cult of dream for stark reality,
the ashes, the dark scarf,

the veils of widowhood;
you are bereft,
accept the accomplished fact;

beyond, beyond, beyond,
when your bare feet
bleed with the salty wrack

of a strange coast,
and your hair hangs,
loosed from its golden snood,

in snaky tangles, lift a stone
and taste the salt of earth, the salt of sea,
and with the stone, strike at your breast and cry,

"alas, alas, mine was the blame,
mine was the guilt";
down, down, down the path of glory,

the Sun goes into the dark,
the Gods decree
that Helen is deserted utterly.

O ebony island, O tall cypress-trees,
now I am blessed anew as my dark veils
cling close and close and make an image of me,

a cypress-Helen, *vierge* and widow, the *femme noire*;
now I am wrapped about
with myrrh and incense,

Egypt's balm and savour
of the burnt Phoenix-nest,
l'île blanche is *l'île noire*;

tighten my bounds,
O unseen and unknown,
wrap me round and round

with Egypt's linen as the dead are wrapped,
mystically cut, cauterise
as with fire, the wound from which

the heart and entrails were drawn out;
a shell? a shattered heart?
no heart is left to heal.

There was a Helen before there was a war,
but who remembers her? O grandam, you, you, you,
with faded hair — you answer, you descend,

ascend, from where? it was all over,
I was wrapped in a tight shroud,
but you appear; the death-bands fall away;

you have come, grandam, no toothless grin,
no *corbeau sur une crâne*;
"remember," you say, "Helen, remember?"

and it is yesterday and the sea-wind flutters my veil,
and my brothers stand side by side,
and my sister weaves the blossoms for my hair —

laughter? how we laughed together,
I had forgotten — there was always stern command
or fear or loss with the others,

or treachery or guilt or subterfuge;
Odysseus had gone and my sister was to marry
or had married Agamemnon,

and "this is no great affair," she confided,
"only laughter, laughter,"
and Menelaus by the altar, whispering,

no stinging, honeyed sigh, but
"it's all right, it's no great matter,
this will soon be over."

Grande Dame, I will carry your crutch for you,
you needn't hobble, hobble any more,
you will tell me what was true,

what wasn't true,
we will walk miles over the sand;
they said, Menelaus came to me in Egypt,

was that true? they said, we lived
on an island somewhere — where?
the legend lives in re-awakened ecstasy,

but I don't think I ever went back to the palace,
the trophies and the banquets, the meeting with Odysseus
when he snatched me away, a second time,

from a dreary round of worldly ceremony;
no, no, I never went back to the world, that world;
I lived in hope of simple consummation,

not a sword — but the labyrinth of Troy
encompassed me — then darkness — Paris slain,
Achilles' heel, the deadly, rumbling chariots,

the shouts, the flames and a voice, *Helen*;
there was a Helen before there was a War,
Menelaus remembered her.

Helios-Helen-Eros? Is that Menelaus?
is that the golden first love, innocence?
is that the Child before the Child was born,

imagined with the cap-crown of bright hair,
inheritance of the "golden Menelaus"?
not Menelaus, but myself gazed up at me,

in the veiled glance of Helen-Hermione;
they said there was a Child in *Leuké*,
they said it was the Child, Euphorion,

Achilles' Child, grandam,
or fantasy of Paris and a Child
or a wild moment that begot a Child,

when long ago, the *Virgo* breasts swelled
under the savage kiss of ravening Odysseus;
yes, yes, grandam, but actually and in reality,

small fists unclosed, small hands fondled me,
and in the inmost dark,
small feet searched foot-hold;

Hermione lived her life and lives in history;
Euphorion, *Espérance*, the infinite bliss,
lives in the hope of something that will be,

the past made perfect;
this is the tangible
this is reality.

The golden apples of the Hesperides,
the brushed-bloom of the pollen
on the wing of ravishing butterfly or plundering bee;

the gold of evanescence or the gold
of heavy-weighted treasure,
which will out-weigh the other?

grandam, great *Grande Dame,*
we will go on together,
and find the way to hyacinths by a river,

where a harp-note sounded
and a moment later —
grandam, great *Grande Dame,* He is here with us,

in notes ascending and descending from his lyre,
your Child, my Child and Helios' Child, no other,
to lure us on, on, on, Euphorion, *Espérance.*

There was a Helen before there was a War,
Odysseus remembered her, so the running away
and hiding in a cave or a forester's hut

was true too, and Taygetus' snow;
but you watched over that Helen, *Grande Dame,*
for Odysseus had his Princess and was never faithful,

and there was Menelaus waiting, for to fulfil
the ultimate decree, Helen must forget Odysseus
and be Sparta's queen;

there was a Helen before there was a War
and Achilles must have remembered her,
hardly a glance, but passing through the palace

with Patroclus, his indifference must have challenged her
with like indifference; for Paris,
there was only the ultimate recognition

and departure, but there was a moment,
standing on the water-stair in the darkness,
when Helen might have wavered,

turned . . .
fighting for her kingdom,
like a tigress;

it was only a moment of indecision,
but there was a Helen before there was a War,
did Paris remember her?

Grandam, midwife, *Sage-Femme,*
let me rest, let me rest,
I can't struggle any more;

far, far, let them beget their children
in the wastes or palaces; what is their happiness,
their bliss to this accomplishment?

Oenone, O, Oenone,
live your life, I need no longer chafe
in fantasy or remembrance or regret;

grandam, midwife, *Sage-Femme,*
I pray you, as with his last breath,
a man might pray, keep *Espérance,*

our darling from my sight,
for bliss so great,
the thought of that soft touch,

would drag me back to life
and I would rest;
grandam, great *Grande Dame,*

midwife and *Sage-Femme,*
you brought Him forth in darkness,
while I slept.

I am delirious now and mean to be,
the whole earth shudders with my ecstasy,
take *Espérance* away;

cruel, cruel *Sage-Femme*,
to place him in my arms,
cruel, cruel *Grande Dame*,

to pull my tunic down,
so Odysseus sought my breast
with savage kiss;

cruel, cruel midwife,
so secretly to steal my phantom self,
my invisibility, my hopelessness, my fate,

the guilt, the blame, the desolation,
Paris slain to rise again
and find Oenone and mortality,

Achilles' flight to Thetis
and the Sea (deserting *Leuké*),
Menelaus with his trophies in the palace,

Odysseus — take the Child away,
cruel, cruel is Hope,
terrible the weight of honey and of milk,

cruel, cruel, the thought of Love,
while Helen's breasts swell, painful
with the ambrosial sap, *Amrita*

that must be given;
I die in agony whether I give or do not give;
cruel, cruel *Sage-Femme,*

wiser than all the regents of God's throne,
why do you torture me?
come, come, O *Espérance,*

Espérance, O golden bee,
take life afresh and if you must,
so slay me.